On Easter Morning

La mañana de Pascua

written by Judy Zocchi

illustrated by Rebecca Wallis

dingles&company New Jersey

First paperback printing

PUBLISHED BY dingles&company

P.O. Box 508 • Sea Girt, New Jersey • 08750

WEBSITE: www.dingles.com • E-MAIL: info@dingles.com

Library of Congress Catalog Card No.: 2004091733

ISBN: 1-59646-194-2

Printed in the United States of America

For Al and Marie

ART DIRECTION & DESIGN Barbie Lambert

EDITED BY Andrea Curley

SPANISH EDITED BY John Page

RESEARCH AND ADDITIONAL COPY WRITTEN BY Robert Neal Kanner

EDUCATIONAL CONSULTANT Anita Tarquinio-Marcocci

CRAFT CREATED BY the Aldorasi family

ASSISTANT DESIGNER Erin Collity

PHOTOGRAPHY BY Sara Sagliano

PRE-PRESS BY Pixel Graphics

Holiday Happenings

examines the
most popular holidays
celebrated by various cultures.
The series explains
the origin of each day
as well as popular traditions
and activities
associated with it.

On Easter morning it is
a tradition to receive a decorated basket
filled with chocolates and candy.

On Easter morning you might wake up and find a basket

La mañana de Pascua puedes despertar y encontrar una canasta

La mañana de Pascua,
es tradición recibir una canasta
decorada y llena de chocolates
y dulces.

The shapes of the
Easter candies say something about
the meaning of Easter. The chick and bunny
are symbols of rebirth. The egglike shape
of jelly beans represents the Easter egg,
which symbolizes renewed life.

filled with chocolate bunnies and chicks.

lena de conejitos de chocolate y pollitos.

Las formas de los dulces de la
Pascua expresan algo sobre el significado
de la Pascua. El pollito y el conejito son símbolos de
renacimiento. La forma oval de los caramelos de goma
representa el huevo de la Pascua, que
simboliza la vida renovada.

And at the bottom
there might be
a jelly bean mix!

¡Y al fondo puede
haber una mezcla
de caramelos de goma!

It is a common practice for Christians to dress up in new clothes and attend a church service to celebrate Jesus Christ rising from the dead.

On Easter morning you could get dressed up

La mañana de Pascua te puedes vestir

Es una costumbre común para cristianos de vestirse en ropa nueva y asistir los servicios de la iglesia para celebrar la resurrección de Jesucristo de entre los muertos.

in a new suit or spring attire.

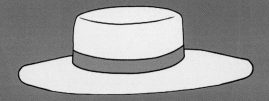

con un traje nuevo
o traje primaveral.

Then you
go to church and sing
in the choir!

¡Luego ir a la iglesia
y cantar
en el coro!

On Easter morning you could visit your grandma

La mañana de Pascua puedes visitar a tu abuela

It is an Easter tradition to give an Easter lily as a gift or to decorate the home or church with them. The lily represents purity, hope, and life, the spiritual ideas of Easter.

and bring her a lily or two.

y traerle un lirio o dos.

Es una tradición de la Pascua de regalar un lirio como regalo o para decorar el hogar o la iglesia con él. El lirio representa la pureza, la esperanza y la vida, las ideas espirituales de la Pascua.

Then you bring her
to the Easter parade
with you!

¡Luego la traes al desfile
de Pascua contigo!

On Easter morning you could
open plastic eggs

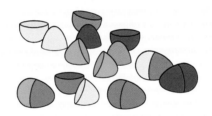

La mañana de Pascua puedes abrir
los huevos de plástico

Easter egg hunts
are popular. Young children
search for and gather eggs
that were hidden in their homes
or yards by their parents
or friends.

to fill with candy and hide.

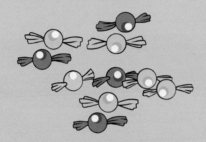

para llenarlos de dulces
y esconderlos.

Las cazas de huevos
de Pascua son populares. Niños
jóvenes buscan y juntan los huevos
que estaban escondidos en sus
hogares o patios por sus
padres o amigos.

Then you invite
your friends to hunt
for them outside!

¡Luego invitar a tus amigos
para ir a la caza
de ellos afuera!

Easter

Easter is a religious holiday that celebrates the resurrection of Jesus Christ. Christians believe that Jesus Christ is the Son of God. They also believe that after he died he rose from the dead. The word "Easter" comes from "Eostre," the name of an ancient goddess of springtime. Easter does not fall on the same day every year. Instead, Easter is celebrated on a Sunday between March 2 and April 25. Today, Easter is celebrated with parades, Easter egg hunts, sending greeting cards, and giving Easter baskets filled with sweets such as chocolate Easter eggs and jelly beans to family and friends.

La Pascua

La Pascua es un día religioso que celebra la resurrección de Jesucristo. Cristianos creen que Jesucristo es el Hijo de Dios. También creen que después de morir, Él resucitó de entre los muertos. La palabra "Easter" viene de Eostre, el nombre de una diosa antigua de la primavera. La Pascua no cae el mismo día cada año. En vez, la Pascua se celebra el domingo entre el 2° de marzo y el 25 de abril. Actualmente, la Pascua se celebra con desfiles, cazas de huevos de Pascua, enviando tarjetas, y regalando canastas de Pascua llenas de golosinas, como huevos de chocolate y caramelos de goma, a familia y amigos.

DID YOU KNOW...

Use the Holiday Happenings series to expose children to the world around them.

- Americans buy 5 million jelly beans for Easter. That's enough to circle the earth three times.
- The most expensive jeweled eggs in the world were made by goldsmith Carl Faberge. The Russian czar Alexander III asked Fabergé to make a special egg for his wife, Marie, in 1885.
- In medieval times, an egg-throwing festival was held in church during Easter. A priest would throw a hard-boiled egg to one of the choirboys, who in turn would toss it to the next choirboy, and so on. The one who was holding the egg when the clock struck twelve was the winner and got to keep the egg.
- Easter is the second largest candy-eating holiday for Americans, who consume about 7 billion pounds of candy.

BUILDING CHARACTER...

Use the Holiday Happenings series to help instill positive character traits in children. This Easter emphasize Respect.

- What does respect mean?
- How do you show respect to your parents/grandparents/friends?
- Why should you respect yourself?
- How does it feel to be disrespected?
- Should you respect nature?

CULTURE CONNECTION...

Use the Holiday Happenings series to expand children's view of other cultures.

- Find out which countries celebrate Easter.
- How do they celebrate the holiday?
- Are these celebrations similar to the way you celebrate Easter?

TRY SOMETHING NEW...

Show respect for your classmates by accepting them just the way they are!

For more information on the Holiday Happenings series or to find activities that coordinate with it, explore our website at **www.dingles.com**.

 **Craft**

Springtime Mosaic Decoration

Goal: To create a springtime decoration using the shells from dyed Easter eggs

Craft: Mosaic springtime decoration

Materials: shells from hard-boiled Easter eggs, plastic sandwich bags, construction paper, crayons or markers, scissors, glue

Directions:

1. Gather materials.

2. As you eat your colored Easter eggs, save the eggshells in plastic sandwich bags. Separate the eggshells by color. Try to peel off the shells in big pieces as this makes them easier to handle. Make sure to peel off all of the film from the backs of the shells.

3. Once you have collected the shells from several different-colored Easter eggs, you are ready to begin.

4. Take a piece of construction paper and draw a springtime shape on it, for example, a flower, a kite, or a butterfly. You can draw your outline in black or whatever colors you chose.

5. Spread glue over the entire picture. Then place different-colored eggshells on the glue. Gently press the eggshells down to be sure they set in the glue. They may rise up a little, so keep checking to see if they need to be pressed down again.

6. Keep gluing down different-colored eggshells until you have filled in the entire shape.

7. Now decorate the background of your mosaic. You can cut out shapes from construction paper such as clouds, birds, and the sun. Then glue them to your picture. (Or, if you prefer, draw the shapes using crayons or markers.)

8. Lay your eggshell mosaic flat until the glue dries.

9. Hang up your mosaic picture to decorate your room for spring!

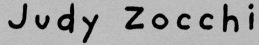

Judy Zocchi

is the author of the Global Adventures, Holiday Happenings, Click & Squeak's Computer Basics, and Paulie and Sasha series. She is a writer and lyricist who holds a bachelor's degree in fine arts/theater from Mount Saint Mary's College and a master's degree in educational theater from New York University. She lives in Manasquan, New Jersey, with her husband, David.

Rebecca Wallis

was born in Cornwall, England, and has a bachelor's degree in illustration from Falmouth College of Arts. She has illustrated a wide variety of books for children, and she divides her time between Cornwall and London.